THE TALK ABOUT COLLECTIONS OF A WRITTEN MIND

Taylur's pen speaks the greatness of God to the broken hearted, the discouraged, and the undecided. As a poetic evangelist, Taylur takes the reader on her journey of discovery: defining her voice and recognizing that her pen has always been anchored in Him. Taylur gives a gentle push forward for aspiring, seasoned authors and poets. I had to slowly re-read her book to get every ounce of goodness.

Collections of a Written Mind is a discourse of awakening; it is a sweet encouragement to those grieving because they have failed to move forward. This book is a gem and will inspire you to pick up your tools to fulfill your purpose. Read this and expect to be delighted in the beauty of her descriptions of God's favor. ~**Leigh K. Ware, D.Min., MSW, BA, CEO and Founder, Leigh K Ware Group, LLC, Lawrenceville, GA**

After reading *Collections of a Written Mind* I stand in awe of the book and the author. This book speaks directly to my spirit and I felt very much a part of these poems. The book brings life and lets the reader know that Jesus is unmovable in this world of issues. There is no doubt that the book showcases Taylur Holland's knowledge and passion for writing. It is easy to feel instantly connected to her writing as the author understands how to engage readers of all ages. I recommend this book for all readers who enjoy any reading genre. ~**Tazetta Walls, Author, *I Am Reflections of Peace*, Founder, Restoring the Walls Ministries, Chicago, IL**

My initial thought of Taylur Holland upon meeting her was that she is young, humble, sweet and pure.

Sometimes when we indulge in a book, movie or song based on the title, we tend to filter its content and our outlook is steered to a particular direction. When I saw *Collections of a Written Mind*, I didn't focus on the title; I simply jumped right into the content. I spent time reflecting after each poem. For me, this book felt like a peek into the very mind of God. Taylur Holland takes you on her personal journey when God removed the veil and made His ways, His heart and His thoughts known to her. Taylur allowed the Lord to write upon the canvas of her heart. Her pen speaks a bold, quiet and confident assurance and reminder that God is your EVERYTHING. **~Sadjah Echols, Co-Pastor, Greater Works International Fellowship, Houston, TX**

The Beginning of a Young
Poet's Journey

TAYLUR HOLLAND

I dedicate this book to my foundation and faithful edification at all times—my family.

I love you.

Collections of a Written Mind—The Beginning of a Young Poet's Journey
by Taylur Holland

Cover design, editing, book layout and publishing services by KishKnows, Inc., Richton Park, Illinois, 708-252-DOIT

admin@kishknows.com, www.kishknows.com

ISBN 978-0-692-15903-3
LCCN 2018909295

All rights reserved. No part of this book may be reproduced, distributed, or transmitted in any form or by any means, including photocopying, recording, digital scanning, or other electronic or mechanical methods, without the prior written permission of the publisher, except in the case of brief quotations embodied in critical reviews and certain other noncommercial uses permitted by copyright law. For permission requests, please contact Taylur Holland.

Copyright © 2018 by Taylur Holland

Printed in the United States of America

Contents

Preface 1
"Speak" 3
"The Rock of All Ages" 6
   The Story Behind the Words 11
"I Am" 14
   The Story Behind the Words 19
"My Child" 20
"Let God Lead" 24
"Found" 28
"The Face of Adversity" 31
"Holy Peace" 34
"God Has Released" 38
"Favor" 42
"Use What is Before You" 45
   The Story Behind the Words 49
"Stooped Low" 51
   The Story Behind the Words 55
"Kind Ignorance" 56
"New" 59
"In and Out" 63
"Righteous Fruit" 67

"Overcome"	71
"Rain"	74
"Nature Has"	79
"God Bless the Tears"	83
"Time"	86
"Remember, Believe, and Know"	89
"Standing in The Middle"	93
"All Yours"	97
"I Am Yours"	101
"Turnaround"	104
"His Song"	108
"In Me...I Have"	111
"Turn Back to Me"	115
"My Ordained Declaration"	119
"The Waters"	123
"Nature"	126
"Dear Brother"	129
"Dear Children"	134
"Please"	138
Excerpt of 14	143
The Next Release from Taylur Holland	143
Introduction	145
Why I Write: A Reflection	149
Author Bio	151
Author Contact Info	155
Acknowledgements	157

Preface

God is my Strength, my Salvation, and my Portion. He is my Inheritance and my Redeemer. I thank God for gracing me with this body of work, and for giving me a voice through the written word. It is my prayer that you will be blessed and encouraged by these words. I pray that these words will be life to you and will stir you to seek and desire God. I pray that every time you open this book, you are refreshed, empowered, and opened to receive all that God has for you.

God is the author, and I, the instrument by which He records the plans of His heart. I am honored to be the vessel through which He will touch, heal, restore, and deliver. He is to be revered in all things and glorified in every way, for He is good and greatly to be praised! Amen.

God bless you,
Taylur Holland

"Speak"

Let Your breath establish a
revelation upon my soul.
Please breathe an unveiling of Your mystery
to my heart, mind, body, and spirit.
Show me an understanding.
Place before me a path I should tread upon.
Let this revelation
have eyes and ears
So that I may see
with a pure sight and
hear with a sensitive ear.
Let Your revelation
breathe life unto me.
Give me a new mind made fresh
and ready to accept Your words.
Speak Lord. Speak Lord.

What does this poem mean to you? In what way can you relate to the words of this poem? Consider, reflect, and use the lines below to write your thoughts.

"The Rock of All Ages"

As I journey through
A clamor of rocks—
Tiny, stony, places of suffering—
I realize that rocks stand firm,
And tell of a land's troubles,
Tell of a land's old age
And of its deepest secrets.
A rock stands firm,
Untouched, unmoved
By the prevailing winds and rains.

In a wrinkle of time,
The rock can't be swayed,
But still stands firm
Telling of the land's history.

The land weeps a sweet cry,
Searching for something longing
In its heart.
The land sings a bitter song,

While trying to seek
What it most desires.

The land, being blind to the apparent light,
Stumbles in the darkness,
While the rock sees all.

The rock, a place of refuge,
And yet also, of remorse.

The land's cries are heard,
While she lifts up her voice and mourns.

She hides in her sorrows of night,
Though what she seeks most is day.

The rock, standing firm,
Can't be moved,
Unless the land and I
Move it.

What does this poem mean to you? In what way can you relate to the words of this poem? Consider, reflect, and use the lines below to write your thoughts.

_____
_____
_____
_____
_____
_____
_____
_____
_____
_____
_____
_____
_____
_____
_____
_____
_____
_____
_____
_____

THE STORY BEHIND THE WORDS

When I began my journey as a poet, "The Rock of All Ages" was the first poem I wrote. I was 14 years old, and I was at a Writers' Club meeting. The other students in attendance were talking about how they had journals of different things they'd written. I considered myself and realized that the only time writing was sparked in me was when a school assignment demanded it. I didn't write just to write. I had always had the ability to write, and I absolutely enjoyed it. However, the idea of walking around with a journal and pen in tow and venturing into woods or onto park benches to write the day's observations hadn't ever crossed my mind. In so many words, I was blown away by what I was hearing. I remember thinking, "I want to try that." As in, "I just want to try to write — to just write." So I did.

A picture formed in my mind:

It was an overcast day, and I saw myself walking on a beach of white rocks.

That's all I saw, and I began to pen "The Rock of All Ages" from that picture. I just wrote what was coming to mind. At that time, I didn't understand what I was writing. I didn't have a structure or know how I should construct each verse. I just wrote, and in "just writing" something was unlocked in me: a passion. A passion I had never before sensed or felt. It was just new. It was as if a whole new world was opening itself up to me—a world that was limitless, a world that I had a place in, a world in which my voice could be found—even if only the paper I was writing upon could hear it.

Prior to me experiencing this moment, writing was birthed from me merely out of obligation. But as I began to venture more into this world of writing poetry, I found that writing was so much more than obligation; it was essential to who I was and how I made sense of life. More years would pass before I truly understood why writing was and is so vital to my life. Simply, it is this: writing bridged me to God.

When I was 20 years old, I came across this poem again and reread it. It was at that moment that I realized this poem was all about Jesus. As I said earlier, when I wrote this poem, I didn't understand what I was writing. I was just going with the flow. After a little more life and time and encounters with God, I was able to look back at this poem and see Him all over it. God was leading me the entire time. At 14, all I had unknowingly done was yield my pen to Him, and He—in the perfection of His sovereignty—took it from there.

"I Am"

My tired hand seeks rest.
My tired heart seeks love.
Why can none be found?
I do all,
Yet I Am not touched.
I see all,
Yet I Am not understood.
In the midst is where I Am,
But who knows?

In the midst, I Am.
In the rain, I Am.
In the sun, I Am.
In the trees, I Am.
In the wind, I Am.
In the heavens, I Am.
Yet who knows?

I give grace and mercy
Every day.

I give heart and life.
I give wisdom.
I Am here before you.
I Am right here—
Arms open wide,
Waiting,
Standing!
Yet who knows?

I give life.
It is I and none other.
I give peace.
Me and none other.
I give direction and understanding—
Me.
I lead,
For I Am God—
Me and none other.

I came, I came, I came.
Me! Me! Me!
It was I.
I comfort, I guide, I lead.
I bless, I give rest.
I build up, I tear down.
I comfort, I give rest, I lead,

For I Am God—
Me and none other.

I Am all that you see before you.
I Am all that is here,
Only Me and none other.
I give peace to the poor.
I give peace to the brokenhearted.
I Am God.
I Am. I was. I Am.
I Am
Today, yesterday, and tomorrow.
I Am God.

What does this poem mean to you? In what way can you relate to the words of this poem? Consider, reflect, and use the lines below to write your thoughts.

_____
_____
_____
_____
_____
_____
_____
_____
_____
_____
_____
_____
_____
_____
_____
_____
_____
_____
_____
_____

The Story Behind the Words

~

I remember the day I wrote this poem. I was in the library at my high school. My last period of the day was a free period, so I would stay in the library to do homework or study or write while I waited for school to end so I could catch the bus and head home. On this particular day, I was writing, and this poem was something different. The words were rushing to my mind, and I was trying to use my pen and paper to capture them as quickly and as best as I could. Then I stopped. I looked up from the paper, realizing that this was not me. I recall thinking to myself, "I don't think like this. I don't talk like this. This isn't me. This is God." This was the first time I recognized that God was the One talking to and through me when I would write. I remember shrugging my shoulders at this realization as I returned to writing. I wrote what I heard, and I didn't stop until the voice stopped.

"My Child"

My child, I see your tears.
My child, I know your longings.
My child, I know your soul is
torn, but your Father is here.
I am the Well
you should drink from—
the Well of Eternal Waters that gives Life and
waters the dusty places.
I am the King.
All you see around you is
My throne.
I am God.
I know your heart is torn.
I know your tears have left you
sore and broken.
You have wept, you have cried,
you have stumbled,
but My dear child, I am God.
I was there all along,
though you saw Me not.

I heard every tear fall,
yet you knew Me not.
Every plea that was cast, I beheld it.
In anguish, your spirit cried out.
It pleaded, it yearned, it longed.
But My dear child, I am God.
I am a God of Restoration.
Though you are broken,
I mend thee.
My child, My dear child, I love you.

What does this poem mean to you? In what way can you relate to the words of this poem? Consider, reflect, and use the lines below to write your thoughts.

"Let God Lead"

When I stand,
Arms outstretched,
Fumbling in the darkness,
Trying to find my way,
I wonder—
Why is it that my way isn't found?
But Lord, You are here to
Hold out Your hand.
When I stumble,
I place my feeble palm
Within great hands of Humility.
Fingers intertwined,
And You lift my head.
You lead, and I follow.

Lord, all that we accomplish
Is because of You.
You deserve all the glory,
For nothing can be done without Your help.
All belongs to You.

So, when I stray in the midst of confusion,
Fumbling through
This thing not of You,
I have to let You lead.
Only then, will I find my way.

What does this poem mean to you? In what way can you relate to the words of this poem? Consider, reflect, and use the lines below to write your thoughts.

"Found"

In difficulty, we find direction.
In adversity, we find peace.
In the breaking—
When we are forced to start over—
We begin, again,
New and refreshed
With a new mindset.
Our mentality has changed,
And order is established.
In times of trouble, we find rest.

What does this poem mean to you? In what way can you relate to the words of this poem? Consider, reflect, and use the lines below to write your thoughts.

"The Face of Adversity"

In the face of Adversity,
What do we see?

Adversity's eyes are cold and gray.
The breath of its open mouth
Presses onward
Seeking to destroy all Hope.
Adversity, a stepping stone
That must be triumphed.

The face of Adversity
Is not but a mask, for under it,
If searched long enough, lies the
Face of Mercy.

Staring into the face of Adversity,
I see Glory.

What does this poem mean to you? In what way can you relate to the words of this poem? Consider, reflect, and use the lines below to write your thoughts.

_____
_____
_____
_____
_____
_____
_____
_____
_____
_____
_____
_____
_____
_____
_____
_____
_____
_____
_____

"Holy Peace"

This is a peace that exceeds
the bounds of our understanding.
There is no limit to this peace,
for this is the Peace of God.
Nothing can be refused
while in this peace.

This peace guards the hearts and
minds of men in Christ Jesus.
It surpasses all understanding.
Impossible becomes Possible
within this peace.

A peace like no other—
such rest cannot be
replaced or copied
or substituted or given by another.

This peace grants all,
gives such rest to all.
It exceeds every bound

and limitation.
It tramples every confine.
It stomps upon the head of worry
and brings the way and
life of tranquility.

All of men's knowledge and
understanding is nothing
compared to this peace,
for it is that of great Holiness.

This Peace of God,
so holy and true.
This Peace of God,
so great and new.
This is the Peace of God
for which I long.

Lord God, give me Peace,
Peace like no other.
Fill me Lord, touch me, restore me,
guard my heart and my mind.
Lord, I am Yours.
Grant me this gift from Heaven.
Holy, Holy, Holy.

What does this poem mean to you? In what way can you relate to the words of this poem? Consider, reflect, and use the lines below to write your thoughts.

"God Has Released"

The rain brought the ideas.
It brought the renewal and
The refreshment—
Such an outpouring of faith
And blessed opportunities.

The rain built puddles of abundance
And shaped the course
That must be traveled.
God has released, and therefore
Replenished,
Restored, and
Refueled.
Again, He has shown up and
Made a way.
Again, He has answered and comforted.

The valiant drops have
Dried the tears and
Erased the painful fears.

God has released an awakening
Of abundance that will
Surpass all doubt and fear
Forever and ever.
The clouds have rolled and clapped.
The thunder has spoken.
The lightning has swept
Across the earth,
And God has released.

What does this poem mean to you? In what way can you relate to the words of this poem? Consider, reflect, and use the lines below to write your thoughts.

"Favor"

Favor is like a spring rain coming
in its due season.
It is like a flower that proudly blooms
once Winter's harsh cry is silenced.
Favor is better than everything
else because it takes care of
everything else.
It allows one to sit back and watch
the wonders of God be created,
formed, and set forth.
Let us walk in favor.
Let us wade in the midst of its
sweet scent.
It has already walked out before
us, so let us follow its lead.
Favor is so cleansing and refreshing
and new and wonderful—
just like a spring rain coming
in its due season.

What does this poem mean to you? In what way can you relate to the words of this poem? Consider, reflect, and use the lines below to write your thoughts.

_____
_____
_____
_____
_____
_____
_____
_____
_____
_____
_____
_____
_____
_____
_____
_____
_____
_____
_____

"Use What is Before You"

Use what bubbles in your ground;
Use what brews in your land.
Turn, and see that God is good.
Turn aside from your
Anguish and despair.
Look to the mountains,
For the Lord our God lives.
He is the Everlasting,
The Mercy, the Grace,
The King, and the Majesty
Forevermore.
Look to Him, and see that
All is well.
He will direct you and guide you,
As He lives,
For eternity and forevermore.
God is King.
Use what is before you.

What does this poem mean to you? In what way can you relate to the words of this poem? Consider, reflect, and use the lines below to write your thoughts.

The Story Behind the Words

When I was in high school, I would print out the prophetic words that God would release through Prophet Kim Clement, put them in a binder, and read them mostly during bus rides to and from school. After reading one of those words, this poem came about. To use what you already have in order to move forward, to advance, and to no longer so desperately rely upon the systems of men to be sustained was impressed upon me in a major way. God was telling us that HE is God. HE is the Creator. HE is our Source. We just need to follow His lead and trust Him. In recent months, I have been reminded of this very thing: "Use what you have." Over and over, this has been coming to mind, and it has encouraged me to push forward, to think outside of the box, and to continue in what God has given me to do. I cannot let what I don't have stop me from trusting God and completing a task or assignment. I just have to use what I do have, trust Him with it all, and keep going. God IS faithful. The question is, are we?

"Stooped Low"

He used to walk upright.
A man with the world at his feet,
The wind at his back,
And the sun in the palm of his hand.
His shoulders sat atop
The greatest kingdoms,
And his hand covered
The whole of the Earth,
But now he walks stooped low,
Having rendered himself to reality.
The pride, worn thin, has left
Him with nothing,
And humility has come to
Keep him stable—
Only so long, only so long.
Pride deteriorates
The realities of time
And gnaws away at the image
Of who one really is.
Only so long does the game last

Before Reality devours Pride and
Leaves one with Nothing.
He knows that now
As he silently walks, stooped low.

What does this poem mean to you? In what way can you relate to the words of this poem? Consider, reflect, and use the lines below to write your thoughts.

The Story Behind the Words

I was 18 and a freshman in college when I wrote this poem. I was walking on campus, and I remember seeing this older man. As he walked, he was slightly bent over, head down. Seeing this man and observing his gait sparked the words to this poem. I imagined that he didn't always walk this way. For some reason, I thought about pride and its adverse effects and deceptions over time, and from these contemplations, this poem was birthed.

"Kind Ignorance"

Ignorance is like a blackened cloud
That passes over the eyes
And leaves one blind.

Ignorance is a mouthpiece
From which your words tread.
Yes, ignorance kindly
Speaks for you.

Ignorance is a deafening silence
That leaves one deaf, and
A curse that leaves no room to bless.
Yes, ignorance kindly intercepts
All the sounds of understanding
From you.

What does this poem mean to you? In what way can you relate to the words of this poem? Consider, reflect, and use the lines below to write your thoughts.

_____
_____
_____
_____
_____
_____
_____
_____
_____
_____
_____
_____
_____
_____
_____
_____
_____
_____
_____

"New"

When New arrives,
Change is stirred, and
Fear is felt.
Old and simple, threatened.
Are we prone to go insane
When something we can't
Understand arrives?

We are afraid of the unusual,
Sickened by the odd, and
Threatened by the different.
We value the usual,
Love the common, and
Kneel at the throne of religion.
We prefer
In with the old, out with the new,
Rather than the reverse.

We'd rather backtrack into
Our past, instead of

Move into our future.
Addicted to yesterday,
Afraid of tomorrow,
Stuck in the present—for now.

Old equals
The sturdy way of life, but
New is inhumane.

What does this poem mean to you? In what way can you relate to the words of this poem? Consider, reflect, and use the lines below to write your thoughts.

_____
_____
_____
_____
_____
_____
_____
_____
_____
_____
_____
_____
_____
_____
_____
_____
_____
_____

"In and Out"

Can we not close our eyes
To the outward—
To the seen
And dream deep? To
Dream worlds of truths and
True beings,
What will it take?
Will it take a veil
Bound in light to reveal the
Most inner thoughts, ways, and truths?
Will it take a loss of one's self to
Understand truly who one is?

The outward should not
Speak for the inward,
But decorate it, shelter it, and
Not conceal it.

It should comfort that which is
Hidden and give it hope.
In and out the world sways.
In dark and in light it waits.
For its sight, it waits.
For its light, it sways in and out.

What does this poem mean to you? In what way can you relate to the words of this poem? Consider, reflect, and use the lines below to write your thoughts.

"Righteous Fruit"

Trembling,
Shaking,
Quaking,
The earth moans for the unknown.
Shivering in the dark.
No need for cold light.
Waiting for many to be revealed,
But tormented until that day.

Where is the fruit that will yield the
Good and calm the strange?
So much one would give and
Offer up.
So much that would be sacrificed
For our common good.
The One, sinless in appearance and Spirit—
The One, Who gave life and
Took the pain.

The earth quaked and moaned.
It hummed a sad song when
this One was given.
Still some wait.
Still some seek.
Where is the righteous fruit?

What does this poem mean to you? In what way can you relate to the words of this poem? Consider, reflect, and use the lines below to write your thoughts.

"Overcome"

You may just have to keep falling
In order to learn how to stand and prevail.
To overcome,
You may have to cry many tears
And lift up many prayers,
But in time, you will triumph.
Don't worry. Don't give up.
You will conquer, and
You will survive.
By God and with God,
You will overcome.

What does this poem mean to you? In what way can you relate to the words of this poem? Consider, reflect, and use the lines below to write your thoughts.

"Rain"

We are right here in the middle
Between shine and rain.
The clouds roll thick,
Yet the sun still shines.
Rain, inviting and full of
Nature's pure fragrance—
It drips with an aroma of truth.
It sweetens the air with
Nature's great perfume.
It caresses the dry place and
Fills every thirst.

Showers of blessings,
Sweet drops of miracles,
Precious morsels of the
Bread of Life
Gracing every lost soul.

This water gives Life to the
Limp and idle.

It breathes Life into
Breathless beings.
Deserted places are filled
With Life and its great flood.
Rain drops of miracles are coming.
The Famine and the Drought
have been laid aside—
This water shall melt away the
Dust and bring
Peace.
All that was taken away shall
be Returned—Doubled.
A great Multitude of Abundance
Shall be poured from
Heaven.

Subtraction has lost its way, and
Multiplication has taken its place.
God has come,
For He is in the Cloud.
The Cloud,
The size of a man's hand—
God is there,
Sending the rain,
Sending the anointing,
Sending the soothing,

Sending the peace,
Sending the grace and the mercy.
God is there.

The waters shall come....
Poured from Heaven,
They will come.
In the floods shall be an overabundance,
Shall be Prosperity,
Shall be God.

In the floods, God will bless—
God will deliver—
God will heal.
He will do all that He has promised,
For nothing is impossible for my God.
I believe and receive in the name of Jesus.
Amen.

What does this poem mean to you? In what way can you relate to the words of this poem? Consider, reflect, and use the lines below to write your thoughts.

_____
_____
_____
_____
_____
_____
_____
_____
_____
_____
_____
_____
_____
_____
_____
_____
_____
_____
_____

"Nature Has"

The sunset breathes down
upon me.
Its rays comfort me.

The snow drifts past,
and its white encompasses me.

The rain has fallen
and has dried every tear.

The wind has dreamt of life.
Far and wide, it has stretched.

The fog has carried secrets,
and the sun has exposed.

Night has fallen
upon the head of doers,
and eager dreamers have
slept instead.

The horizon has melted away fears,
and the bronzed sky has whispered.

The dew of morning beckons
in the night.
For its time it weeps.

Summer follows the
hand of Spring.
Fall pursues the
heart of Winter.

Earth, wind, fire, air.
Nature has its way.

Through it, God shares grace
and spares the hearts of men.

Nature has overcome.

What does this poem mean to you? In what way can you relate to the words of this poem? Consider, reflect, and use the lines below to write your thoughts.

"God Bless the Tears"

Tears are the stories of my thoughts.
My expression, my heart, my soul
flowing in a steady stream.
I seek for them to cease,
but my story must be told.
For that moment, for that time,
it must be heard.

My tears are the answers to the
mysteries stranded inside of me.
Sometimes, they betray the
façade of a calm demeanor
and unlock the story
written within me.

They release my most inner feelings
and fail to be restrained.
My tears, my stories, my life
sown into the showers that
drip from my sight.
God bless the tears.

What does this poem mean to you? In what way can you relate to the words of this poem? Consider, reflect, and use the lines below to write your thoughts.

_____
_____
_____
_____
_____
_____
_____
_____
_____
_____
_____
_____
_____
_____
_____
_____
_____
_____
_____

"Time"

As time is watched,
It consumes an eternity.
It becomes a glacier that lethargically melts.

As my eyes stare into
the face of time,
Its hand wanly waves at my anticipation.
Time is a gracious thing.

What does this poem mean to you? In what way can you relate to the words of this poem? Consider, reflect, and use the lines below to write your thoughts.

"Remember, Believe, and Know"

Child, lift up your head and see the sun.
Lift up your face and hear your awakening.
Open your eyes and taste your destiny.
Walk with your feet and feel your future.
Open your mouth to bear
witness of your call.
Once you have sensed its
precious scent,
forget not that I made you, and I called you.
Forget not that I knew you
above all.
Drift not into the realms of oblivion
and become unaware of My presence.
Seek after Me and pursue your desire.
I will quench it,
but you must first delight in Me.
Believe that I Am—
that what I have begun, I have also finished.

It
is done.
Believe and know.
Remember, and do not forget.
Embed this truth into your
memory, and
live.

What does this poem mean to you? In what way can you relate to the words of this poem? Consider, reflect, and use the lines below to write your thoughts.

"Standing in The Middle"

As I stand in the middle,
On behalf of many,
God, I pray You hear my request.
I shed tears and cry for others
As if their tears were my own,
For this compassion flows deep.
God, please lend Your ear to my Spirit
And hear.
Shed Your holy grace.
Give Your humble mercy.

When I stand in the middle,
I thank You, Lord, for being
My God,
For hearing me when I call.
Lord, I pray, keep me stayed
upon Your being
So when I whisper Your holy name,

You will accept my
Intercedent offering.

If I cry for one, I will cry for all,
For I carry their stories with me,
And their every struggle has
Become mine also.

When I stand in the middle,
It is their tears that
Drop from my eyes.

When I stand in the middle,
The words that You have graced me
To pray on their behalf
Flow from my lips.

When I stand in the middle,
Lord, I pray, that my heart and
My life are pure in Your sight.

Please accept my
Interceding offering.

What does this poem mean to you? In what way can you relate to the words of this poem? Consider, reflect, and use the lines below to write your thoughts.

"All Yours"

No room to take credit,
For we are so indebted
    To You.

It's all Yours.
Everything established
In Your name.
A word released from Your lips
Created night and day.

From Your voice,
We in this world were formed.
God, it is all Yours.

Water from a rock.
My refuge, joy, and stronghold.

Twelve months
Four seasons
Seven continents

Four oceans
Twelve sons
Twelve stones

Twelve signs painted in the skies—
An unfaltering foundation all
Pointing back to You.
It's all Yours.

Everything
Established by Your voice. Lord,
It is all Yours.

What does this poem mean to you? In what way can you relate to the words of this poem? Consider, reflect, and use the lines below to write your thoughts.

"I Am Yours"

In the wind,
You called my name.
Before I even had a face,
You called my name.
Cold winds pressing,
You knew me.
Before I was birthed,
Still in the womb,
It was me You knew.
For all days and all ages,
I was here.
In existence, in time, I was.
Eternal, afloat, in the realm
of eternity, I was.
Where did I lay, and where
did I make my bed?
Where did I drift and see You?
Me, You have known for all days.
I am Yours, my King and Savior,
I am Yours.

What does this poem mean to you? In what way can you relate to the words of this poem? Consider, reflect, and use the lines below to write your thoughts.

"Turnaround"

Up and down
I've gone.
Left and right.
Fettered between right and wrong.
To stand, to sit,
To walk, to run.
To talk, or behold silence.
To go, or to come.
So many choices
And indecisiveness.
One door closes.
Many more open.
A tear falls,
Yet laughter calls.
A broken heart.
A renewed start.
An outspoken voice quieted,
Yet still a trembling voice of fire.

So far up and down
I've gone.
Yet this turnaround,
Is now my beautiful song.

What does this poem mean to you? In what way can you relate to the words of this poem? Consider, reflect, and use the lines below to write your thoughts.

_____
_____
_____
_____
_____
_____
_____
_____
_____
_____
_____
_____
_____
_____
_____
_____
_____
_____

"His Song"

When He gives a song—
A melody anointed by His touch,
Mountains tremble at the voice of an angel.
Trees bow down at His throne.
Chains are broken,
And souls delivered
When His song is sung.

What does this poem mean to you? In what way can you relate to the words of this poem? Consider, reflect, and use the lines below to write your thoughts.

"In Me…I Have"

I will give you strength
and wise counsel.
In Me, you shall find strength and life.
I will direct
and guide you.
I will give you wisdom
and insight.

In Me, there is no imperfection,
for I am in control
and already know the way
I have designated for you.
I have prepared your place
before you.

In the presence of your enemies,
I have made your way straight.
I am your Comforter—
Jehovah Rohi—
in all My great delight.

You shall no longer thirst
or hunger,
but find your rest in Me,
For I have fulfilled your needs.
I am King—
El Shaddai—
mighty in all My stature.
I bring peace and salvation—eternal
gifts from the heavenlies,

Before time, I was.
After time, I will be.
Alpha, Beginning, End, Omega.
Last, First.
Former things have been already.
I dictate even Time's way
and the journey he must cross.

To God be the glory
Forever! Amen.

What does this poem mean to you? In what way can you relate to the words of this poem? Consider, reflect, and use the lines below to write your thoughts.

"Turn Back to Me"

Rain, coming and going.
Dews, lost in the scents
of mourning.
Cry no more, My dear.
Be satisfied and uplifted.

Come to Me, and see clearly.
I am your Way,
your Peace and Answer.
You have gone through,
but I have overcome.

Trust in Me, and obey.
Even those against you will
have peace with you,
for you have chosen Me.
Drift, linger, shower hope.
Give grace and wisdom.
Everlasting love is the
crown upon My head.

Do not cry. Seek after Me.
I am the Way.
Everything
is within My hand and strength.
I will restore you.
Turn.
Turn back to Me.

What does this poem mean to you? In what way can you relate to the words of this poem? Consider, reflect, and use the lines below to write your thoughts.

_____
_____
_____
_____
_____
_____
_____
_____
_____
_____
_____
_____
_____
_____
_____
_____
_____
_____
_____
_____

"My Ordained Declaration"

Don't cry, My child.
I gave you a voice—
A voice to challenge,
A voice to question,
A voice to adhere to My mind,
My thoughts, My ways.

I gave you a say and
The right to speak
Your mind and
To challenge and
To question and
To wisely doubt.

You will not take
This way for this and
That way for that.

Just because Man says right is right
Does not mean that
I have declared it so.

Man says left,
I say right
Because I have ordained it to be.

I have ordered the way
And declared it to be straight.
I am and always will be.
I am above all things.
In Me, there is no fault,
For I have made it so.

I am God and none is like Me.
I am God now and forever.
Call.
I am here.
Right here.

I have declared it to be My way.

What does this poem mean to you? In what way can you relate to the words of this poem? Consider, reflect, and use the lines below to write your thoughts.

"The Waters"

We cry, cleansing.
We cry, refreshing.
We cry, replenishing.
Our body's waters,
Deep and everlasting,
True and so new.

Instilled from the beginning.
What is their path,
The course they must run?
Are they meant to fill us in our times
Of distress and mere agony?
Is their purpose only to wash
Away, remove, and restore?

To God be the glory!
To Him that established the waters
In the high and low places—
Even in our midst—
Thank You, Lord.

What does this poem mean to you? In what way can you relate to the words of this poem? Consider, reflect, and use the lines below to write your thoughts.

"Nature"

Nature is God's drawing board.
It's His way of telling His story.
The wind—
Heard,
Felt, but not touched.
Unseen.
Just like God.
You just know that it's there.
By faith you know.
It's just common,
Just natural to know that it's there.
It's nature.
You can hear God.
You can feel Him, but not
Physically touch Him.
You can't see Him, yet you know He is there.
Just like the wind.
By faith, you just know.
By faith.
By faith
All things are possible.

What does this poem mean to you? In what way can you relate to the words of this poem? Consider, reflect, and use the lines below to write your thoughts.

"Dear Brother"

Dear brother:
Do not destroy.

Dear brother:
Do not fear.

Dear brother:
In God is peace and joy,
for He did not breathe into
us the spirit of fear.

Dear brother:
I call out to you because I see.
You're searching, you're enduring;
please do not crumble beneath
the pressures of this world and earthly realm.
God is in control, He's at the helm.

Dear brother:
Open your eyes and
give Him a chance.

Dear brother:
He has need of you—
that you may fulfill
His righteous plan.

Dear brother:
In God there is nothing but truth.

Dear brother:
A soft ear and sound mind,
love, marked by favor,
holy and divine,
is God's remarkable nature.
He is King forevermore,
High Priest in all His glory.
He wants you, He loves you.

Dear son of Mine,
Turn back to Me.
I have not forsaken you,
nor have I forgotten you,
But I have called you, Son.

I have appointed you to do
all that I ask,
to perform with a willing
heart and spirit
My commands forevermore.
My son,
I love you.

Dear brother, dear brother:
Turn back to Him.

What does this poem mean to you? In what way can you relate to the words of this poem? Consider, reflect, and use the lines below to write your thoughts.

"Dear Children"

Little children, speak.
Little children, endure.
Take heed to My voice and
My Great command.

Little children, speak.
Raise up your voices, and declare My word.
Be not afraid.
Believe that I Am, I Was, I Am
Now, I Will, and I Will Be.

I am the Most High.
The utmost in supremacy.
I am here.
I am God forevermore,
Established on high in
Peace and tranquility.

My Word will not turn void.
In My Word is life and prosperity,

The wealth of hope and security.
Humble is My name,
And might, My wholeness.

Answer Me.
Beckon unto My call, My way, and My light.
Take heed.
Hear My voice,
Little children, and be not afraid.
I am God Most High.

What does this poem mean to you? In what way can you relate to the words of this poem? Consider, reflect, and use the lines below to write your thoughts.

_____
_____
_____
_____
_____
_____
_____
_____
_____
_____
_____
_____
_____
_____
_____
_____
_____
_____
_____

"Please"

Words so profound,
So deep in knowledge,
Spoken,
Yet heard.
Waiting.
I'm giving life.
Can you see not?
I'm speaking joy.
Can you hear not?
Please see.
Please hear.
Please trust Me—
Even when you cannot comprehend
My way.
Question not My focus,
But believe.
I am here.
I am the One
Open, willing, ready to give—
Ready to save.

Open your heart unto Me.
Please.
I am right here.
Tarry not, but come to Me.

What does this poem mean to you? In what way can you relate to the words of this poem? Consider, reflect, and use the lines below to write your thoughts.

EXCERPT OF 14

The Next Release from
Taylur Holland

INTRODUCTION

The Inner Vow

I had just hung up the phone. I stood near the steps that led down into the media room and considered the conversation I had just had. She was a friend—well, now, more of an acquaintance. I had told her about something my thirteen-year-old self was incredibly excited about. I now don't recall what it was, but I know it was something important—important to me. Her response was vague and unfulfilling. She didn't share the same enthusiasm, and I learned firsthand that what is sacred and important to me will not always be sacred and important to others. At the age of thirteen, that disappointment was enough to make me decide to never share anything with anyone ever again. In that moment, I made an inner vow to not speak and share with others what mattered to me.

I didn't want to feel that rejection again. However, God had a plan of His own; and, one year later, at fourteen, I found my voice again. I found it in poetry, and I didn't know just how loudly my voice would speak.

14

At fourteen, I found
my voice in poetry.
She was hidden
amongst a beach of white
rocks and an overcast sky
in November.
I called that place
The Rock of all Ages.

Words.

They became my best
friends.
I would talk to them
in class when history lessons
bored me.
I would rather observe classmates
and write their stories.

Words.

Since I couldn't paint, sketch, or sculpt,
I would strive to construct
pictures with them—
write a vivid photograph,
scribe a colorful image,
pen a portrait
that would help people see what
I saw when I looked at them—
purpose.

Words.

At fourteen, without
map or compass, words
bridged me to Him.

Words.

At fourteen, words saved
my life.

WHY I WRITE: A REFLECTION

For me, writing is essential. It's as important to me as breathing. There were times when I considered putting the pen down. What I would write was unorthodox. There were times when I didn't understand it, and I would question if others would be able to understand it. A lot of my writing would land on God. Even in moments of feeling so apart from Him and empty, my writing would still draw me to Him. With words and sentences, I would go looking for Him. I was anchored in Him—even when I didn't know it, even when I couldn't feel it, and especially when I couldn't see it. How could God still love and care for me so? I didn't know Him as Daddy. I couldn't fathom His mercy. I didn't know that I was His choice. So, God, in all of His wonder and splendor, gave me writing. He placed writing so deep inside of me that it's no wonder that the thought of giving writing up would make my breath stop short. I write because it tethers me to Him—my Source, my Lifeline, my Everything, my very Breath.

Author Bio

Taylur Holland is a spoken word poet with the anointing of the scribe on her life. She started writing poetry at fourteen years old, and it has always been her desire for people to know peace, healing, answers, and restoration when they experience her writings.

Since the debut of her first book of poetry, *Come Forth*, Taylur has had the opportunity to share her poetry across multiple platforms. Her work has been featured in magazine publications, and she was even selected as the Featured Artist for a magazine which is dedicated to honoring and celebrating artists and their creativity. Also since *Come Forth*, Taylur has pioneered two movements with messages that she spreads through clothing and apparel: *Writer Write* and *I Was Delivered to be a Deliverer*. The *Writer Write* movement is all about empowering writers to respond to the mandate on their life, and simply, write. For every time the *Writer Write* message is seen and worn, Taylur's prayer is that the witness and the wearer are stirred to write and release the words they have been given for the earth. The *I Was Delivered to be a Deliverer* movement was birthed from a moment in which Taylur was invited to freestyle rap at a conference event. That declaration—*I Was Delivered to be a Deliverer!*—was made during the rap, and it resonated with those in attendance. So Taylur created a shirt bearing that message, a shirt that serves to remind the wearer that the story of what they have overcome and survived will never be in vain—that they survived in order to go back and get someone else free.

Along with these opportunities, Taylur's greatest joy has come from those moments in which she has been invited to speak at youth programs and schools. In her words, "*Tay Tay luh da kids,*" and Taylur has found that she is most rewarded when she has the chance to speak into, impact, empower, and encourage the lives of the youth. She desires for them to know that they are valuable, that they have a purpose, and that they are never too young to serve He Who created them—for He is so worth serving. She looks forward to more of these moments with the youth—especially as she prepares to venture into the world of music. Stay tuned.

To learn more about Taylur and to stay in the know about what she's up to, visit www.taylurholland.com, where you can sign up to receive emails about her upcoming projects.

Author Contact Info

Website: www.taylurholland.com

Facebook: www.facebook.com/taylurholland

Twitter: www.twitter.com/taylurholland

Instagram: www.instagram.com/taylurholland

YouTube: www.youtube.com/thescribesheart

For booking information or inquiries, please email: info@thescribesheart.com

Acknowledgements

~

To God, my Father, my Keeper, my Lord, my Savior, my Hope, my Strength, my Redeemer, my Peace, my Joy, my Answer, my King—thank You. Thank You for trusting me. Thank You for keeping Your hand stayed upon my life, for saying *"Yes"* to and over me long before I knew I could articulate a *"Yes"* back to You. You have kept me from the beginning. You have loved me for even longer. God, thank YOU. Lord, I love You, forever and always. Lord, forever and always.

To my family, thank you for your constant edification. You strengthen me. You impart wisdom into me. You cover me. You pray for me. You watch over me. You help me. You love me. You see what I can't always see. You bring a balance so anchored in the wisdom of the Lord. You encourage me to not only do all of what God has placed inside of me to do, but even more so, to live uprightly before Him and wholly serve Him. Thank you. More and more, thank you. I really don't know where I would be without all of you, and I am just so thankful to God for blessing me to be a part of this family. I love you so so much.

To my friends, thank you for coming alongside me and daring to push me into destiny. Thank you for so sincerely helping me to birth God-given visions and ideas into the earth as if they were your own. I am honored to have people in my life who have upright hearts, who genuinely desire to see me do what God has entrusted me to do. Thank you for your prayers. Thank you for reaching out to me. Thank you for your friendship. Thank you for just loving me. God gives good gifts, and I thank Him for giving me each one of you. I love you dearly.

www.ingramcontent.com/pod-product-compliance
Lightning Source LLC
Chambersburg PA
CBHW071926290426
44110CB00013B/1497